UTAH

BY ANN HEINRICHS • ILLUSTRATED BY MATT KANIA

The **Child's World**®
childsworld.com

Published by The Child's World®
1980 Lookout Drive • Mankato, MN 56003-1705
800-599-READ • www.childsworld.com

Photo Credits

Photographs ©: Shutterstock Images, cover, 1, 23, 28, 38 (top), 38 (bottom); James Van Couver/iStockphoto, 7; Benny Marty/Shutterstock Images, 8; Maria Jeffs/Shutterstock Images, 11; Robert Ingelhart/iStockphoto, 12; Randy Judkins/Shutterstock Images, 15; Everett Historical/Shutterstock Images, 16; iStockphoto, 19, 20, 35; James St. John CC2.0, 24; Doc Searls CC2.0, 27; Andre Jenny Stock Connection Worldwide/Newscom, 31; Stuart Blyth/iStockphoto, 32

ISBN 9781503819849
LCCN 2016961196

Printing

Printed in the United States of America
PA02334

Ann Heinrichs is the author of more than 100 books for children and young adults. She has also enjoyed successful careers as a children's book editor and an advertising copywriter. Ann grew up in Fort Smith, Arkansas, and lives in Chicago, Illinois.

post card

About the Author
Ann Heinrichs

Matt Kania loves maps and, as a kid, dreamed of making them. In school he studied geography and cartography, and today he makes maps for a living. Matt's favorite thing about drawing maps is learning about the places they represent. Many of the maps he has created can be found in books, magazines, videos, Web sites, and public places.

post card

About the
Map Illustrator
Matt Kania

On the cover: Take a hike through Bryce Canyon National Park.

OUR UTAH TRIP

Are you ready to tour the Beehive State? That's Utah. You'll be busy as a bee on this trip! Just wait and see.

You'll hike through deep **canyons**. You'll float in a lake and never sink. You'll learn about **pioneers** and railroads. You'll watch miners dig copper from the ground. You'll tour a candy factory and eat roasted lamb. And you'll see some ancient rock art!

There's a lot to do, so let's get going. Just buckle up and hang on tight. Utah, here we come!

WELCOME TO
UTAH

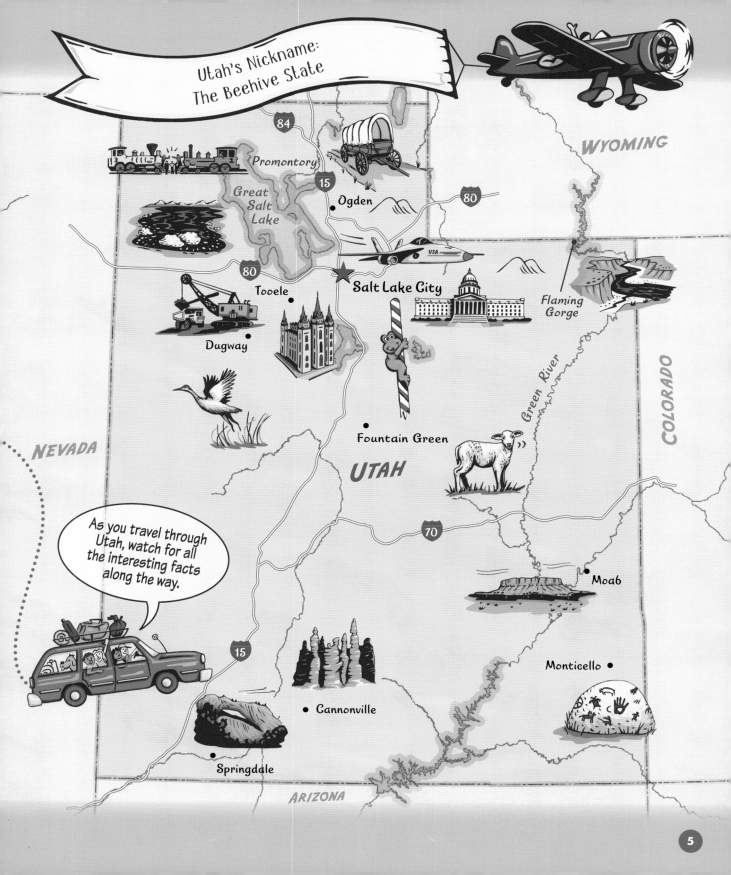

Lowest Temperature: Peter Sinks February 1, 1985 −69°F (−56°C)

IDAHO

WYOMING

Peter Sinks •

Let's take a hike through the hoodoos! We might see some chipmunks and horned lizards!

Great Salt Lake Desert

Great Salt Lake

Wasatch Range

Uinta Mountains

Kings Peak

NEVADA

• Wendover

★ Salt Lake City

Highest Temperature: Saint George July 5, 1985 117°F (47°C)

Utah's many mountain ranges are part of the Rocky Mountains. One is the Uinta Mountains in northeast Utah. Another is the Wasatch Range. It rises east of Salt Lake City.

Rocky Mountains

Green River

The Bonneville Salt Flats are near Wendover. Race-car drivers test their speeds there!

Moab •

Colorado River

COLORADO

Washington County

Saint George •

• Cannonville

ARIZONA

HIGHEST AND LOWEST POINTS HIGHEST: Kings Peak at 13,528 feet (4,123 m) LOWEST: Washington County at 2,000 feet (610 m)

The Paiute called the Bryce Canyon rock formations "Legend People."

6

Thousands of weirdly shaped rocks loom overhead. They're called hoodoos or goblin rocks. You're exploring Bryce Canyon National Park! It's in southern Utah, near Cannonville.

Utah has many strange, colorful rock formations. Wind and water carved them over the years. The Rocky Mountains cover much of the state. Some mountains are snowcapped all year long.

The Green River runs through eastern Utah. It joins the Colorado River near Moab. Western Utah is very dry. The Great Salt Lake is in the northwest. Nearby is the Great Salt Lake Desert.

What amazing shapes! Don't forget to visit Bryce Canyon!

FUN IN FLAMING GORGE

There's so much to do in Flaming Gorge! Swoosh down the **reservoir** in a canoe. Brightly colored canyon walls rise around you. Explore the rock walls on foot. You'll see ancient rock art from the Fremont. Or hike the Canyon Rim Trail. You'll spot wildlife among the red rock mountains.

There's plenty to do outdoors in Utah. People enjoy boating, fishing, hiking, rock climbing, and skiing. Flaming Gorge and Glen Canyon are popular spots. Do you like bike riding? Then try mountain biking!

Don't forget your life jacket! Visitors can paddle through Flaming Gorge.

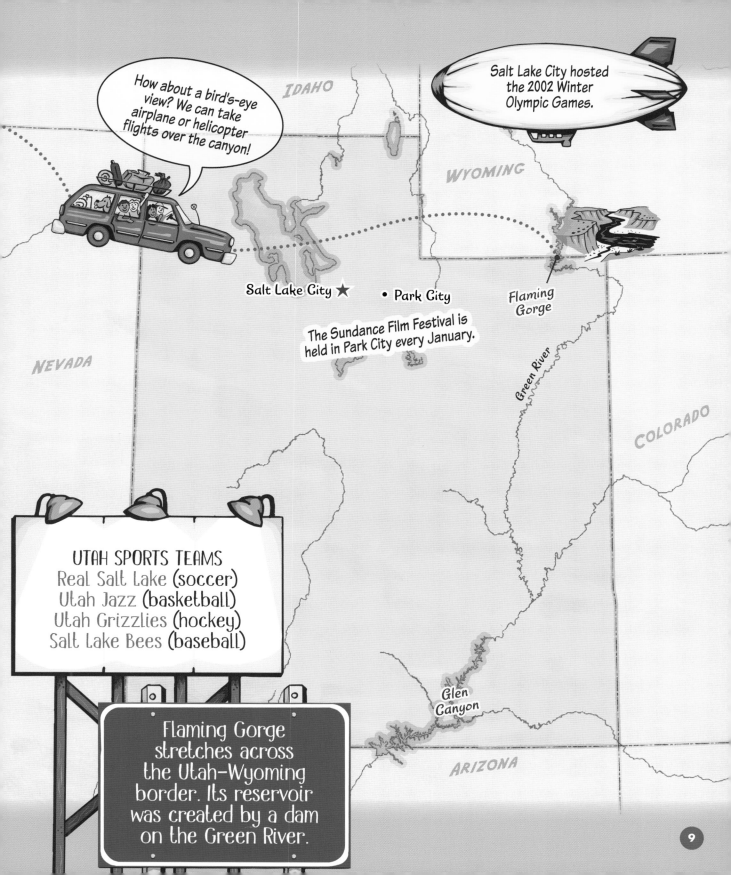

Fish Springs National Wildlife Refuge is at the southern end of the Great Salt Lake Desert.

STATE FLOWER
SEGO LILY

STATE TREE
BLUE SPRUCE

STATE BIRD
CALIFORNIA GULL

WYOMING

Great Salt Lake Desert

Dugway

NEVADA

Ever hear of Lake Bonneville? It used to cover this whole area. Fish Springs evolved only approximately 11,400 years ago.

COLORADO

Delta

Bighorn sheep and mountain goats live in Utah's mountain regions.

Delta holds the Snow Goose Festival in late February and early March. Thousands of big, white snow geese stop in the area to feed then.

Why is the seagull Utah's state bird? In 1848, crickets swarmed across Utah. They might have eaten all the crops. But flocks of seagulls flew in and ate the crickets!

The National Park Service has 17 sites in Utah.

You see herons, egrets, rails, and cranes. These long-legged birds wade in the water. They catch fish and gulp them down!

You're visiting Fish Springs National Wildlife **Refuge** in Dugway. Deserts are all around this refuge. But the refuge itself is a wetland. It gets its water from underground springs.

Thousands of birds nest and feed here. There are ducks, geese, eagles, and owls. Lots of other animals live in Utah. They include coyotes, jackrabbits, antelopes, and mule deer. Cacti and other hardy plants grow in Utah's deserts. Forests cover some of the mountains. But watch out! Bears and mountain lions hide out there.

American Coots are just one of the many birds that call Fish Springs home.

Can you read Newspaper Rock? It's covered with pictures, not words. There are people, animals, and strange objects. They're petroglyphs, or art, carved into rock. Ancient people carved them hundreds of years ago. The pictures are like a newspaper. They tell about many events and activities.

The Anasazi people carved most of these pictures. The Anasazi once lived in southern Utah. Some built homes high on the rock cliffs. Others built pueblos, or villages, many stories high. The Fremont were another early group. Their homes were pits dug into the ground.

There are more than 650 ancient drawings at Newspaper Rock.

IDAHO

WYOMING

NEVADA

Who Lived Here before Europeans Arrived?
Anasazi, Fremont, Gosiute, Navajo, Paiute, Shoshone, and Ute

Is that a wheel? Is that a 6-toed foot? Is that a giant lizard?

COLORADO

Hovenweep National Monument, near Bluff, continues into Colorado. People lived there more than 10,000 years ago. Ruins of homes and towers still exist.

The Edge of the Cedars State Park Museum in Blanding has Anasazi artifacts.

• Boulder

• Monticello

• Blanding

• Bluff

Anasazi State Park Museum is in Boulder. People lived there from approximately 1050 to 1200 AD. The site's museum displays objects that were uncovered there.

ARIZONA

Anasazi ruins can be seen at Cedar Mesa and Grand Gulch, west of Blanding.

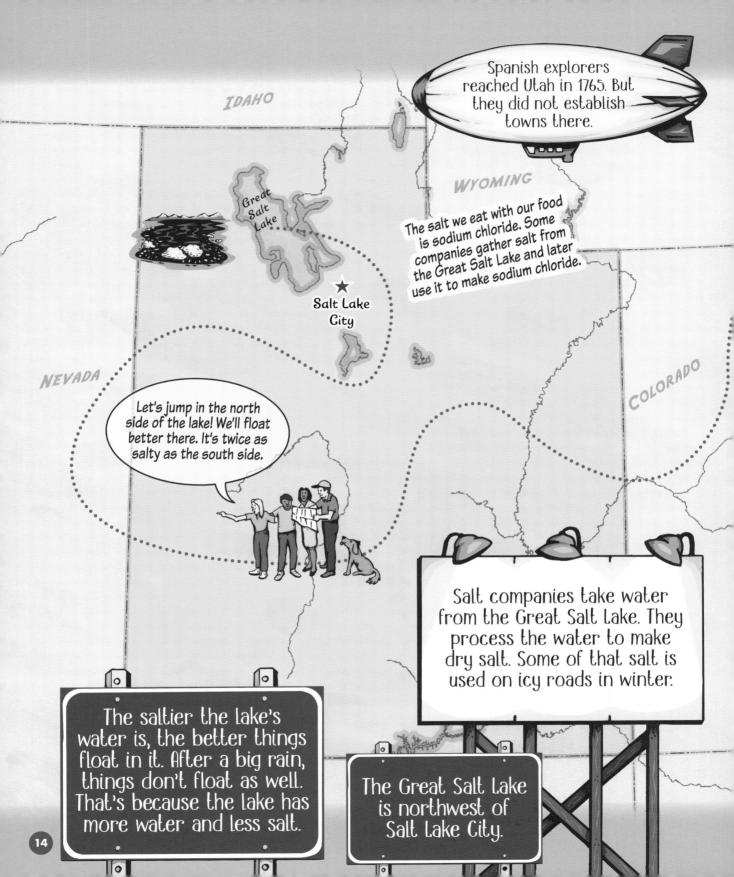

THE GREAT SALT LAKE

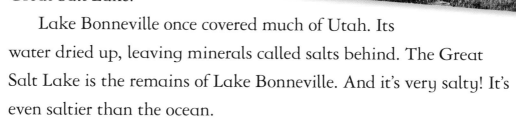

Float in the lake without fear. You won't sink! But try not to swallow the water. It's so salty that you might choke. It's the Great Salt Lake!

Lake Bonneville once covered much of Utah. Its water dried up, leaving minerals called salts behind. The Great Salt Lake is the remains of Lake Bonneville. And it's very salty! It's even saltier than the ocean.

Jim Bridger reached the lake in 1824. He might have been the first white person there. But some people also say a fur trader named Etienne Provost might have been the first. When Bridger arrived, he tasted the salty water. He thought he'd reached the Pacific Ocean!

Bridger was a fur trapper and scout. Many other trappers soon arrived in Utah.

Take a moment to relax. Try floating in the Great Salt Lake.

PIONEER DAYS IN OGDEN

Kids are marching with decorated wagons and bikes. Covered wagons are rolling along. It's the Pioneer Days parade in Ogden!

Pioneer Days celebrates Utah's first white settlers. Brigham Young led them there in 1847. They all belonged to the Mormon religion. They were seeking religious freedom.

Most of the settlers had traveled from Illinois. It was a long, hard journey. They walked with handcarts or rode in covered wagons. By 1869, approximately 70,000 Mormons were in Utah. They built **irrigation** systems across the dry land. Then they could grow many crops.

Brigham Young became governor of the Utah Territory in 1851.

July 24 is Pioneer Day in Utah. It honors July 24, 1847, when Brigham Young and his followers arrived in the Salt Lake valley.

The Mormon settlers fought the Ute, led by Chief Black Hawk. The Black Hawk War lasted from 1865 to 1867.

Oh, boy! They've got a horse parade, too! Cowboys, soldiers, and mountain men are all riding their horses.

The town of Bountiful holds Handcart Days in July. It honors the settlers who walked to Utah, pulling or pushing all their belongings in handcarts.

The Mormons called their new homeland Deseret, meaning "honeybee." The honeybee is a symbol of hard work. That's how Utah got its nickname, the Beehive State.

Salt Lake City holds the Days of '47 celebration every summer. It honors Utah's 1847 settlers.

Utah is named after the Ute people who lived in the area.

IDAHO

WYOMING

NEVADA

COLORADO

Ogden •

• Bountiful

★ Salt Lake City

If you dropped a pin in the Mormon Tabernacle while it's very quiet, you can hear the sound ringing through the building!

West Valley City • ★ Salt Lake City

• Provo

The Joseph Smith Memorial Building is in Temple Square. People can explore their roots at its Family History Library.

In 2016, 3,051,217 people lived in Utah. It's the 31st-largest state by population.

Mormons belong to the Church of Jesus Christ of Latter-day Saints. The church is sometimes called LDS (Latter-day Saints) for short.

Joseph Smith (1805-1844) was the founder of Mormonism. He published the *Book of Mormon* in 1830. This is the holy book of the Mormon faith.

POPULATION OF LARGEST CITIES
Salt Lake City................192,672
West Valley City...........136,208
Provo.............................115,264

SALT LAKE CITY'S TEMPLE SQUARE

You cannot miss Temple Square. It's Salt Lake City's most famous site. The Mormon Salt Lake Temple stands at one end. It's a beautiful house of worship. The public may not go inside, though.

Nearby is the Salt Lake Tabernacle. Its organ and choir are world famous. Also in Temple Square is the Beehive House. Brigham Young lived there in the 1800s.

Many more buildings stand in Temple Square. They all relate to Mormon history and activities. Salt Lake City is the Mormon church's world center. Today, the Mormon faith is strong in Utah. Approximately six in ten residents are Mormons.

Learn about the Mormon religion by visiting the beautiful Temple Square.

Utah's state capitol is full of history lessons. The lessons are all in pictures! Just stand in the rotunda. That's the tall, rounded space under the dome. The wall paintings show historical scenes. They include many early explorers. And you'll see Brigham Young and his pioneers.

This building houses Utah's state government offices. Utah has three branches of government. One branch consists of the state lawmakers. Another branch makes sure laws are carried out. The governor heads this branch. The third branch is made up of courts. Judges rule over the courts. They decide whether laws have been broken.

See the lawmakers hard at work in the state capitol.

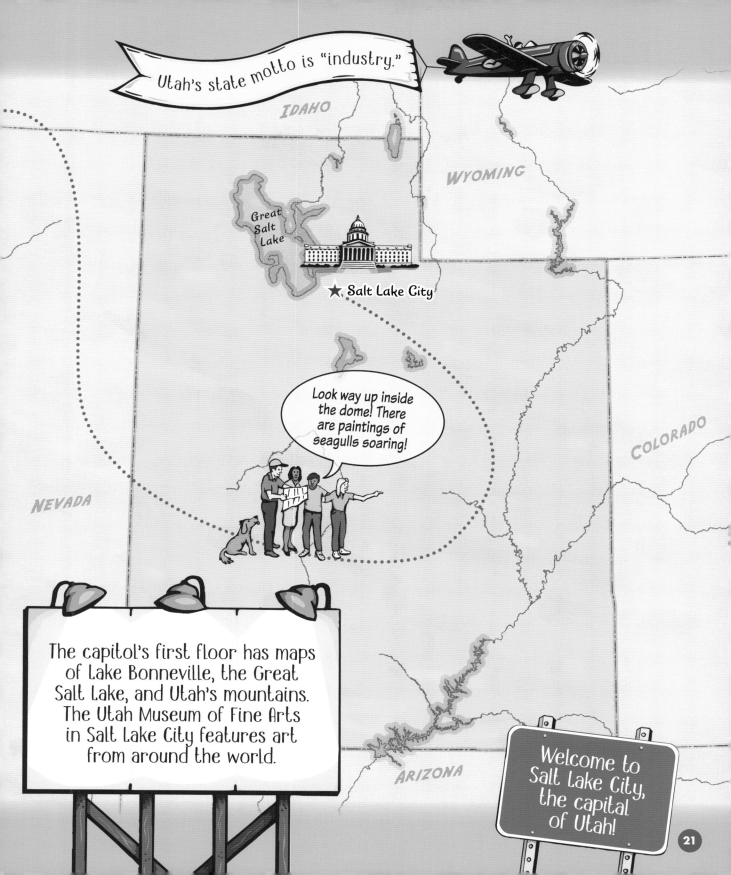

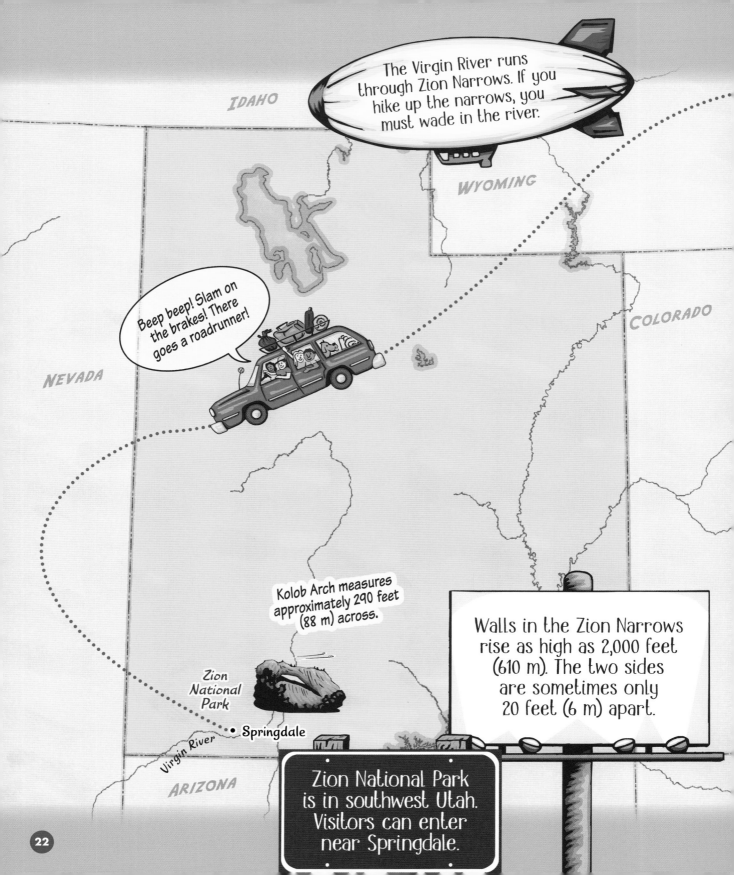

EXPLORING ZION NATIONAL PARK

Zion National Park is an awesome place. It's full of towering cliffs and deep canyons. Its rock formations are pink, red, and orange.

Mormons first settled this area in the 1860s. They gave it the Hebrew name *Zion*. That means "a place of safety and rest."

What can you do in Zion National Park? You can hike! Many people hike the Zion Narrows. Its towering rock walls are very close together. The park's Kolob **Arch** is a famous site. It may be the world's largest natural arch.

Do you like watching wildlife? You'll see lots of animals in the park. There are bighorn sheep and mountain lions. There are roadrunners, too!

Hike along the cliffs at Zion National Park in Springdale. Don't look down if you're afraid of heights!

PROMONTORY'S GOLDEN SPIKE

Ching, ching! People are swinging enormous hammers. They're hammering gigantic **spikes**. What's going on?

It's the Golden Spike Ceremony! This event first took place in 1869. People act it out every year in Promontory.

The Golden Spike was a big, gold railroad spike. It joined the last section of the transcontinental railroad. The railroad stretched across the whole country.

Some workers built tracks heading west. Others built tracks heading east. The two sections met in Promontory. The Golden Spike was hammered in. Then everyone cheered!

All aboard! You can see train replicas from the 1800s in Promontory.

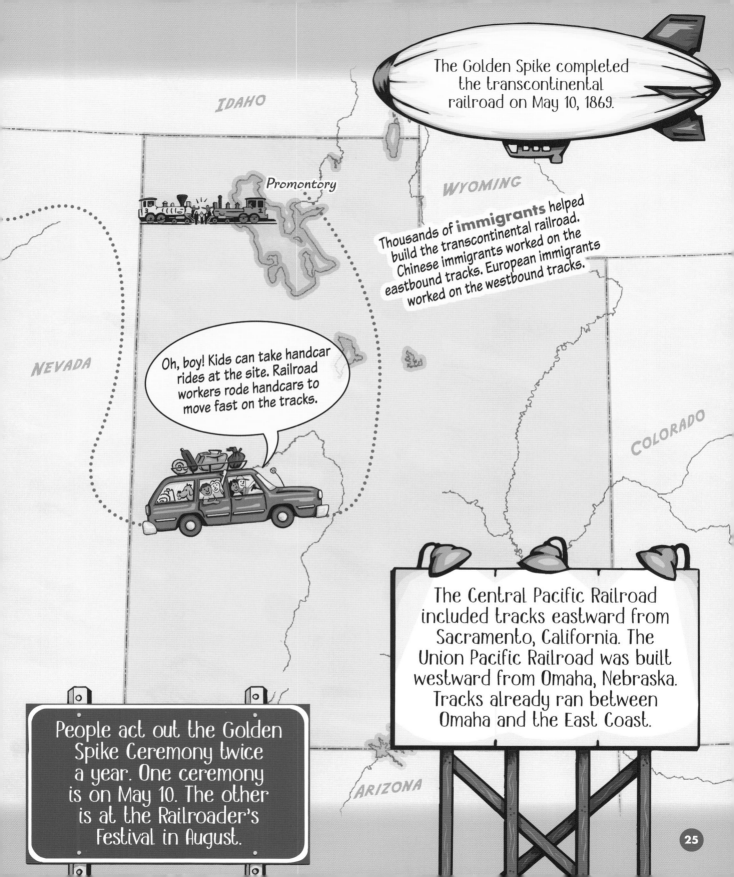

The Golden Spike completed the transcontinental railroad on May 10, 1869.

Thousands of **immigrants** helped build the transcontinental railroad. Chinese immigrants worked on the eastbound tracks. European immigrants worked on the westbound tracks.

Oh, boy! Kids can take handcar rides at the site. Railroad workers rode handcars to move fast on the tracks.

The Central Pacific Railroad included tracks eastward from Sacramento, California. The Union Pacific Railroad was built westward from Omaha, Nebraska. Tracks already ran between Omaha and the East Coast.

People act out the Golden Spike Ceremony twice a year. One ceremony is on May 10. The other is at the Railroader's Festival in August.

IDAHO

Promontory

WYOMING

NEVADA

COLORADO

ARIZONA

Utah was the 45th state to enter the Union. It joined on January 4, 1896.

What's made with copper? Lots of stuff! Electrical wires and water pipes, for example.

• Tooele

The first library books were carried to Utah by oxen in the 1850s.

Pennies used to be made mostly of copper. Now they're zinc coated with a small amount of copper.

What's Mined in Utah? Petroleum, copper, coal, and natural gas

Copper mixed with zinc makes brass. Copper mixed with tin can make bronze.

The Kennecott mine yields more than copper. Gold, silver, molybdenum, and other metals are mined there, too.

VISITING KENNECOTT COPPER MINE

Look over the railing at Bingham Canyon. You're looking down into a massive pit. Huge trucks are hauling chunks of copper **ore**. They dump the ore into a crusher. It crushes the ore into smaller pieces. How small? Approximately the size of soccer balls!

You're visiting the Kennecott copper mine near Tooele. Mining became a big **industry** in Utah. Southeastern Utah had rich coal deposits. Coal mines dotted this region in the 1880s. Other areas were known for their iron, silver, gold, and lead.

Copper mining became important in the 1890s. The Bingham Canyon area is rich in copper. It's one of the world's top copper producers today.

Visit the Kennecott copper mine to find out how copper is mined.

TOURING KENCRAFT CANDIES

Kettles are boiling the syrupy goo. Then workers put it into the stretching machine. Each gooey glob is bent, twisted, and cut. Next, watch the candy artists. They add decorations in sugary colors. What's the final product? Candy sticks, candy canes, and suckers—yum!

You're touring Kencraft. It's a candy factory in American Fork. Food products are among Utah's many factory goods. Some food plants make yummy snacks—such as candy!

Metals and computers are also made in Utah. Some factories make parts for missiles and rockets. Others make air bags for cars. Medicines are Utah products, too.

Treat your sweet tooth at Kencraft.

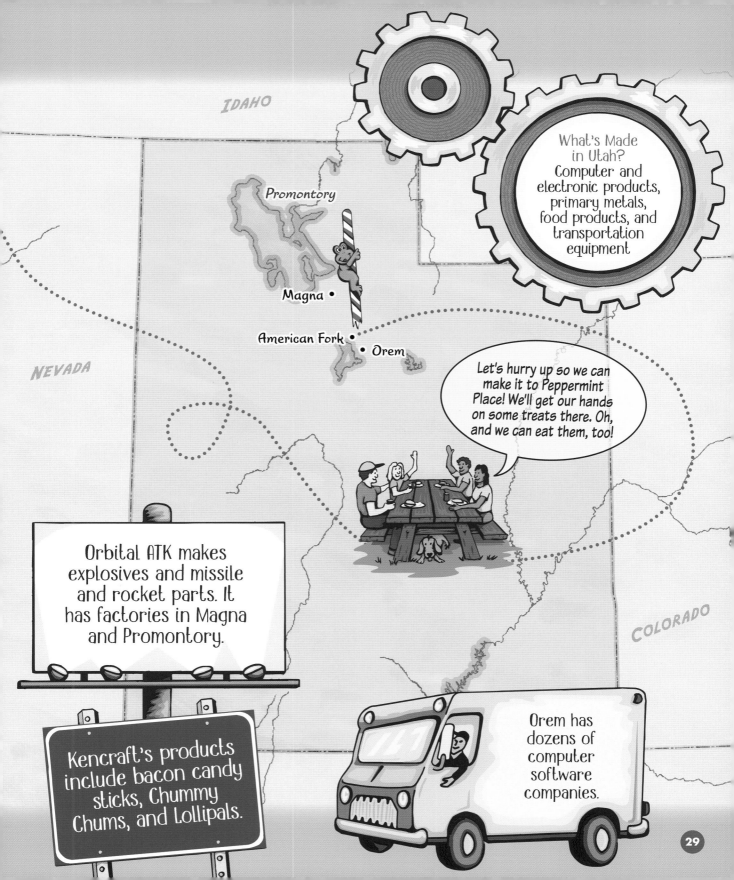

IDAHO

Promontory

Magna •

American Fork •

• Orem

NEVADA

COLORADO

What's Made in Utah?
Computer and electronic products, primary metals, food products, and transportation equipment

Let's hurry up so we can make it to Peppermint Place! We'll get our hands on some treats there. Oh, and we can eat them, too!

Orbital ATK makes explosives and missile and rocket parts. It has factories in Magna and Promontory.

Kencraft's products include bacon candy sticks, Chummy Chums, and Lollipals.

Orem has dozens of computer software companies.

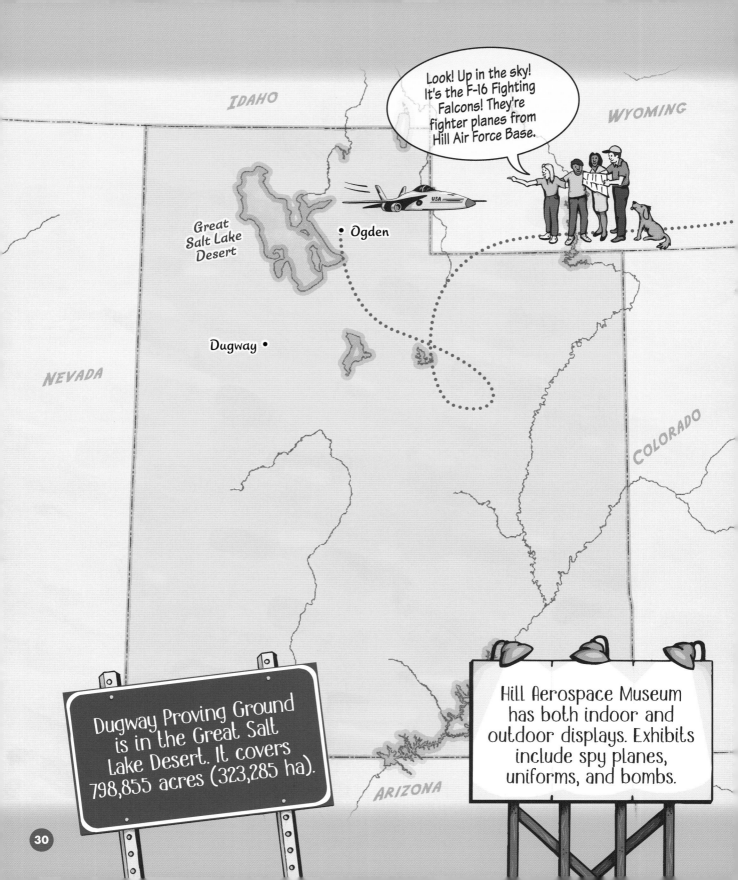

HILL AEROSPACE MUSEUM

Check out Hill **Aerospace** Museum. You'll see lots of military airplanes. Some have snarly faces painted on them!

This museum is on Hill Air Force Base. It's just south of Ogden. The aerospace industry is important in Utah.

Wendover Range was busy during World War II (1939–1945). Airplanes practiced dropping bombs there. Dugway Proving Ground opened in 1942. It's still a military testing site. In the 1950s, Utah began building missiles. Utah still makes parts for missiles, rockets, and spacecraft.

Would you like to be a pilot? Take a tour of Hill Aerospace Museum!

LAMB DAY IN FOUNTAIN GREEN

Kids are dressed as lambs for the parade. Lamb is roasting in big barbecue pits. People are racing in the Lamb Scram. It's Lamb Day!

Lamb Day is a big festival in Fountain Green. It celebrates the region's sheepherding history. Utah is a leading state for raising sheep. Beef and dairy cattle are valuable, too. They produce tons of meat and milk. Many farmers also raise hogs and chickens.

Hay is Utah's leading crop. Most of it is fed to cattle. Some farmers raise cherries, apples, strawberries, and peaches. These fruits make great desserts!

Baa! Many Utah farmers raise sheep.

Pleasant Grove holds the Strawberry Days Festival every June.

Most of Utah's farmland is watered by irrigation.

IDAHO

The state fair is held in Salt Lake City in September each year.

WYOMING

NEVADA

Wow, look at all those sheep! It must be Lamb Day!

★ Salt Lake City

• Pleasant Grove

• Fountain Green

COLORADO

Lots of people in Utah own horses. The state holds many rodeos, horse races, and horse shows.

Immigrants from Denmark settled in the Fountain Green area. They came in the 1870s and 1880s. They made a living as sheepherders.

ARIZONA

What Does Utah Raise? Beef and dairy cattle

Utah had approximately 30,695 farms in 1935. Today, the state has approximately 18,000 farms.

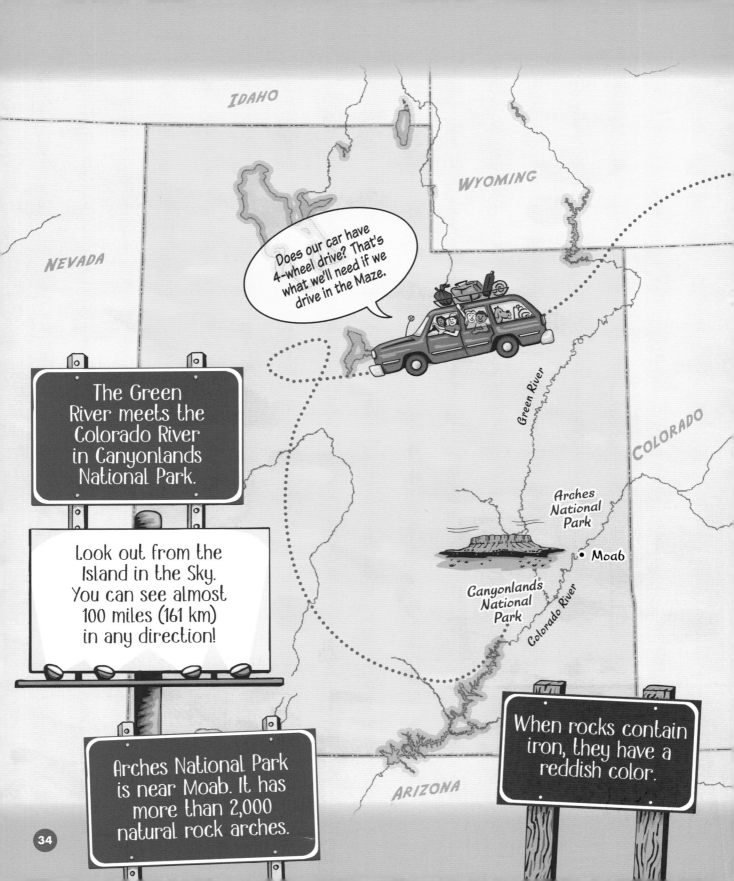

IDAHO

WYOMING

NEVADA

Does our car have 4-wheel drive? That's what we'll need if we drive in the Maze.

Green River

COLORADO

The Green River meets the Colorado River in Canyonlands National Park.

Arches National Park

Look out from the Island in the Sky. You can see almost 100 miles (161 km) in any direction!

• Moab

Canyonlands National Park

Colorado River

Arches National Park is near Moab. It has more than 2,000 natural rock arches.

ARIZONA

When rocks contain iron, they have a reddish color.

THE WONDERS OF CANYONLANDS

What is the Island in the Sky? What are the Needles and the **Maze**? They're all rock formations in Canyonlands National Park. It's Utah's largest national park.

It took millions of years to form Canyonlands. Rivers washed through it. The earth's crust shifted there, too. Layers of rock formed and washed away. What is left today? A jumble of fantastic rock formations!

The Island in the Sky is well named. Its colorful rocks rise high atop a mesa. The Needles are tall, pointy rocks. The Maze is a really wild area. Its canyons are like a rocky puzzle. Be careful, and don't get lost!

Want to see some cool rock formations? Head to Canyonlands National Park!

OUR TRIP

We visited many amazing places on our trip! We also met a lot of interesting people along the way. Look at the map below. Use your finger to trace all the places we have been.

Where is the Sundance Film Festival held? *See page 9 for the answer.*

When did Fish Springs evolve? *Page 10 has the answer.*

Where in Utah can Anasazi ruins be seen? *See page 13 for the answer.*

Who takes water from the Great Salt Lake? *Look on page 14 for the answer.*

Who was Joseph Smith? *Page 18 has the answer.*

What's on the first floor of Utah's capitol? *Turn to page 21 for the answer.*

What is copper mixed with zinc? *Look on page 26 for the answer.*

How many farms does Utah have? *Turn to page 33 for the answer.*

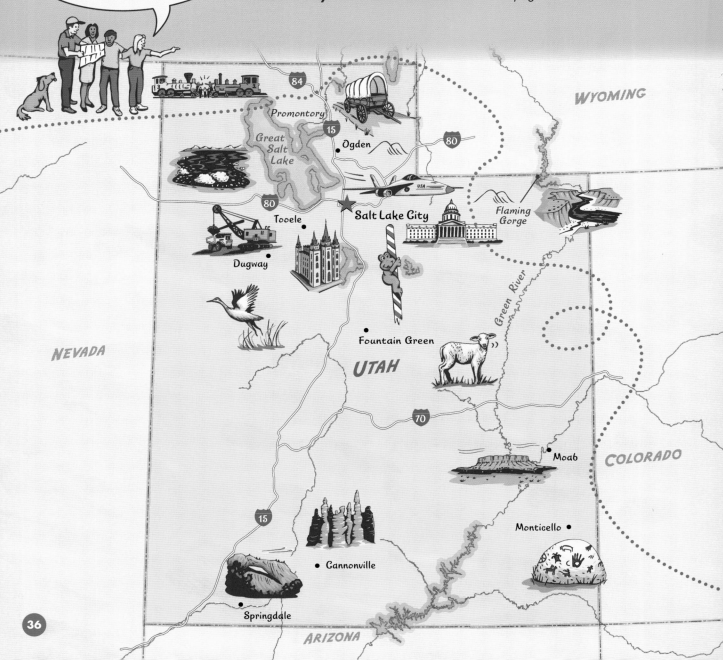

WYOMING

Promontory

Great Salt Lake

Ogden

Tooele

Salt Lake City

Flaming Gorge

Green River

Dugway

NEVADA

Fountain Green

UTAH

Moab

COLORADO

Monticello

Cannonville

Springdale

ARIZONA

STATE SYMBOLS

State animal: Rocky Mountain elk
State bird: California gull
State cooking pot: Dutch oven
State emblem: Beehive
State fish: Bonneville cutthroat trout
State flower: Sego lily
State folk dance: Square dance
State fossil: *Allosaurus*
State fruit: Cherry
State gem: Topaz
State grass: Indian ricegrass
State historic vegetable: Sugar beet
State insect: Honeybee
State mineral: Copper
State rock: Coal
State star: Dubhe
State tree: Blue spruce
State vegetable: Spanish sweet onion

STATE SONG

"UTAH . . . THIS IS THE PLACE"

Words by Sam Francis and Gary Francis, music by Gary Francis

Utah! People working together
Utah! What a great place to be.
Blessed from Heaven above.
It's the land that we love.
This is the place!

Utah! With its mountains and valleys.
Utah! With its canyons and streams.
You can go anywhere.
But there's none that compare.
This is the place!

It was Brigham Young who led the pioneers across the plains.
They suffered with the trials they had to face.
With faith they kept on going till they reached the Great Salt Lake
Here they heard the words . . . "THIS IS THE PLACE!"

Utah! With its focus on family,
Utah! Helps each child to succeed.
People care how they live.

Each has so much to give.
This is the place!

Utah! Getting bigger and better.
Utah! Always leading the way.
New technology's here . . .
Growing faster each year.
This is the place!

There is beauty in the snow-capped mountains, in the lakes & streams.
There are valleys filled with farms and orchards too.
The spirit of its people shows in everything they do.
Utah is the place where dreams come true.

Utah! With its pioneer spirit.
Utah! What a great legacy!
Blessed from Heaven above.
It's the land that we love.
This is the place!

Utah! Utah! Utah!
THIS IS THE PLACE!

That was a great trip! We have traveled all over Utah. There are a few places that we didn't have time for, though. Next time, we plan to visit the Tracy Aviary in Salt Lake City. Visitors can see more than 135 kinds of birds there. They can even attend classes, shows, and camps to learn more about Utah's birds.

FAMOUS PEOPLE

Cannon, Martha Hughes (1857–1932), first female state senator

Cassidy, Butch (1866–ca. 1908), outlaw

Farnsworth, Philo (1906–1971), inventor

Fullmer, Gene (1931–2015), boxer

Garn, Jake (1932–), former U.S. senator who became the first U.S. member of Congress to fly in space while in office

Hough, Derek (1985–), professional dancer

Hough, Julianne (1988–), professional dancer and actress

Malone, Karl (1963–), former basketball player

Ogden, Peter Skene (1794–1854), fur trader and explorer

Redford, Robert (1937–), actor and director

Stegner, Wallace (1909–1993), author

Stockton, John (1962–), former basketball player

Tiegen, Chrissy (1985–), model and TV personality

Walkara (ca. 1815–1855), Timpanogo chief

Wells, Emmeline (1828–1921), Mormon leader and feminist

Young, Brigham (1801–1877), Mormon leader

Young, Steve (1961–), former football player

State flag

WORDS TO KNOW

aerospace (AIR-oh-spayss) relating to air and space flight

arch (ARCH) a curved structure above some sort of opening

canyons (KAN-yuhnz) deep valleys worn away by rivers

immigrants (IM-uh-gruhnts) people who leave their home country and move to another country

industry (IN-duh-stree) a type of business

irrigation (ihr-uh-GAY-shuhn) a human-made system of bringing water to farms through ditches

maze (MAYZ) a confusing network of pathways

mesa (MAY-suh) a high, flat-topped hill

ore (OR) rock that contains valuable materials such as iron or gold

pioneers (pye-uh-NEERZ) people who move to an unsettled land

refuge (REF-yooj) a place of safety and protection

reservoir (REZ-ur-vwar) a human-made lake

spikes (SPIKES) large, heavy nails used to fasten rails to railroad ties

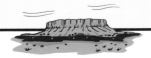

State seal

TO LEARN MORE

IN THE LIBRARY

Felix, Rebecca. *What's Great about Utah?* Minneapolis, MN: Lerner Publishing, 2015.

Marsh, Carole. *I'm Reading about Utah.* Peachtree City, GA: Gallopade International, 2014.

Marsted, Melissa. *Buzzy and the Red Rock Canyons: Utah's National Parks.* Park City, UT: Lucky Penny Press, 2016.

ON THE WEB

Visit our Web site for links about Utah:
childsworld.com/links

Note to Parents, Teachers, and Librarians: We routinely verify our Web links to make sure they are safe and active sites. So encourage your readers to check them out!

PLACES TO VISIT OR CONTACT

Utah Office of Tourism
visitutah.com
300 N. State Street
Salt Lake City, UT 84114
800/200-1160
For more information about traveling in Utah

Utah State Historical Society
heritage.utah.gov/history/historical-society
300 S. Rio Grande Street
Salt Lake City, UT 84101
801/245-7225
For more information about the history of Utah

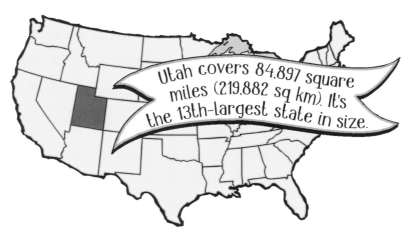

Utah covers 84,897 square miles (219,882 sq km). It's the 13th-largest state in size.

INDEX

Bye, Beehive State.
We had a great time.
We'll come back soon!